Contributors

Kristina Rienzi
Katherine Hutchinson
CC Robinson
Tricia Copeland
Michael Hingson and Keri Wyatt Kent
Roger Lelie
James Hill
Michiel Hoek
Kelly Florence & Meg Hafdahl
Rathan Krueger
Patrick O'Brien
Caroline Lavoie
Tristan Zelden
Robert S. d'Arcy
Carla Kessler
Florence Wetzel
Art Willis
Michael Mohr
Andi Wiseman
Patti Smith

Review Tales
A Book Magazine For Indie Authors

Founder & Editor in Chief: S. Jeyran Main
Publisher: Review Tales Publishing & Editing Services
Print & Distribution: Ingram Spark
Designs: Pexels
ISBN 978-1-988680-58-3 (Paperback)
ISBN 978-1-988680-59-0 (Digital)
www.jeyranmain.com
For all inquiries, please contact us directly.

Photo Credits from Pexels:
pexels-656120440-19859577
pexels-alteredsnaps-18275570
pexels-josh-hild-1270765-4256852
pexels-olenkabohovyk-3646172

Editor's Note

Hello Again,

Welcome to the second edition of *Book Review Magazine*, your go-to magazine for book reviews that spotlight the extraordinary talents of writers from around the globe. After the resounding success of our first edition, we are thrilled to bring you another carefully curated selection of books from the many submissions we've received. Our writing community is brimming with creativity and passion, and it's an honor to showcase the voices that make this world a better place—one story at a time.

Compiling this edition has been an adventure in itself! From breathtaking thrillers to heartwarming memoirs, every book chosen for these pages has something special to offer. It's like walking through a literary carnival—every turn surprises you with new colors, intriguing ideas, and unforgettable characters.

We also sincerely thank the authors who trust us to share their hard work. You inspire us with your words, perseverance, and ability to turn ideas into stories that connect us all. This magazine is a celebration of you and the magic you create.

Whether you're here to discover your next favorite book or revel in the joy of the written word, we hope this issue brings you as much pleasure as we had in creating it. Happy reading!

Warm regards,
Jeyran Main
Editor-in-Chief, Review Tales

Jeyran Main

Editor-in-Chief
Review Tales Magazine

Welcome

WINTER 2025 | ISSUE 02

BOOK REVIEWS

Review Tales is thrilled to have reached the milestone of over 1,900 book reviews. With this extensive experience, we've had the privilege of exploring a vast range of literature. Our reviews are always impartial and thoughtfully crafted to highlight authors' strengths while inspiring them to keep creating. For this Winter issue, we've handpicked 20 exceptional book reviews to feature.

TO APPLY FOR A BOOK REVIEW VISIT
WWW.JEYRANMAIN.COM

Book Reviews

5 HAPPY CHOICES
KRISTINA RIENZI

Reviewer: Jeyran Main

5 Happy Choices: The Simple Way to a Happier Life by Kristina Rienzi is an uplifting and practical self-help book designed to help readers unlock their happiness through five simple, actionable choices. As a bestselling author and certified professional coach, Rienzi uses her expertise to present an accessible guide that empowers individuals to take charge of their well-being and choose happiness every day.

The book's premise is straightforward: happiness is a choice that can be cultivated through deliberate actions. Rienzi focuses on five specific choices, each aimed at shifting the reader's mindset and behaviors to foster lasting happiness. Rather than overwhelming readers with complex theories or jargon, she offers simple, relatable advice that can be easily implemented daily. Each chapter is dedicated to one of the five choices, breaking them into practical steps that encourage immediate action.

What makes 5 Happy Choices stand out is its combination of simplicity and depth. Rienzi's approach is grounded in scientific research, providing a solid foundation for her advice. By incorporating psychological principles, she shows readers how each of the five choices is supported by evidence that they can genuinely improve their happiness and well-being. This evidence-based approach adds credibility to her message and reinforces the practical strategies she shares.

The book is also written in a warm, empathetic tone, making it feel like a conversation with a trusted friend. Rienzi's supportive voice encourages readers to embrace the process of choosing happiness and offers reassurance when challenges arise. She addresses common obstacles such as fear, self-doubt, and uncertainty, providing helpful strategies to overcome these barriers.

In conclusion, 5 Happy Choices is a powerful guide for anyone looking to live a more joyful and fulfilling life. With clear, actionable steps, scientific backing, and relatable wisdom, this book is an invaluable resource for readers ready to make positive changes. Kristina Rienzi's inspiring message proves that happiness is within reach, and the simple choices we make every day can lead to a brighter, more fulfilling future.

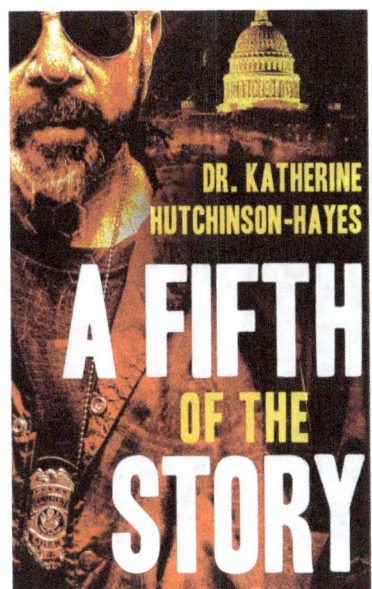

A FIFTH OF THE STORY
Dr. Katherine Hutchinson-Hayes

Reviewer: Jeyran Main

A Fifth of the Story by Dr. Katherine Hutchinson-Hayes is a captivating, fast-paced thriller that expertly blends espionage, action, and psychological depth. The novel follows Brock, a dedicated CIA agent who finds himself caught in a complex and dangerous web of conspiracy after an attack on U.S. soil. What begins as a routine investigation quickly escalates into a life-threatening situation as Brock discovers that one of his closest allies is secretly involved in a terrorist organization planning a catastrophic strike.

Dr. Hutchinson-Hayes masterfully builds suspense throughout the story, keeping readers on the edge of their seats as Brock races against time to thwart the plot. The stakes couldn't be higher as Brock must navigate a labyrinth of shifting loyalties, hidden agendas, and moral dilemmas. His mission is made even more urgent by the need to protect his loved ones, including his field officer's family, who are caught in the crossfire.

What sets A Fifth of the Story apart is its nuanced portrayal of the psychological and emotional toll that espionage and betrayal take on its characters. Brock's internal struggles—his battle between duty and personal loyalty, his sense of duty as an agent, and his desire to protect those he loves—add complexity to the action-driven plot. The author skillfully humanizes Brock, making him more than just a typical action hero. Readers are drawn into his journey not only because of the high-stakes plot but also because of the personal cost he endures.

The novel's pace is relentless, with constant twists and turns that heighten the tension. Dr. Hutchinson-Hayes has crafted a story that combines suspense, action, and emotional depth seamlessly. As Brock uncovers the truth behind the conspiracy, readers keep guessing until the end.

In conclusion, A Fifth of the Story is a must-read for fans of espionage thrillers. With its gripping plot, complex characters, and emotional depth, this book stands out in the genre. Dr. Hutchinson-Hayes delivers a thrilling ride that will leave readers eagerly anticipating the next chapter in Brock's journey.

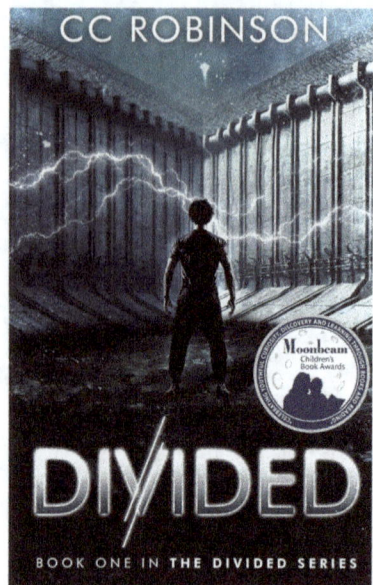

DIVIDED: BOOK ONE IN THE DIVIDED SERIES
CC Robinson

Reviewer: Jeyran Main

Divided: Book One in the Divided Series by CC Robinson is a powerful and gripping dystopian novel that will captivate Divergent and The Hunger Games fans. With its fast-paced action, deeply drawn characters, and a compelling plot filled with tension and intrigue, this book is a must-read for anyone who enjoys a story of rebellion and survival in a harsh, divided world.

The story is set in the Federated Republic of America, where a ruthless dictator, Supreme Commander Martin, holds absolute power over a divided society. Eighteen-year-old Marcos Sanchez is trapped in this oppressive regime under the tight control of his father. His only hope is escape, which seems impossible—until a fateful move lands him in a secret labor camp. There, he meets a group of rebels known as The Underground, who are determined to overthrow Martin's tyrannical rule.

Robinson's impressive world-building creates a dystopian society that feels familiar and terrifyingly real. The towering walls surrounding Queenstown symbolize the division between the privileged and the oppressed, and the tension is palpable throughout the story. As Marcos becomes embroiled in The Underground's plans, he must confront the brutality of Martin's regime and the challenges of trust, loyalty, and sacrifice. Marcos's relationships with his friends, particularly his diverse group of companions in the Underground, add a human element to the story, showing the strength of unity in the face of adversity.

The novel excels in its balance of thrilling action and emotional depth. Robinson doesn't shy away from the harsh realities of the character's world, and the stakes feel high from start to finish. With unexpected betrayals, heart-pounding moments, and a relentless pursuit of freedom, Divided is a story that keeps readers on the edge of their seats. The twists and turns will leave readers wondering who they can trust as the rebels' mission reaches its breaking point.

In conclusion, Divided is a standout novel in the YA dystopian genre. Its well-developed characters, thrilling plot, and thought-provoking themes make it a must-read. Fans of dystopian fiction will find themselves eagerly awaiting the next installment in the series.

KINGDOM OF EMBERS
TRICIA COPELAND

Reviewer: Jeyran Main

Kingdom of Embers: Extended Finale by Tricia Copeland is a captivating start to the Kingdom Journals series, blending elements of urban fantasy, vampire lore, and witchcraft. This first book introduces seventeen-year-old Alena Scott, a complex character forced to navigate life as a vampire-witch hybrid in a world where secrecy is paramount. Her existence is a delicate balance between hiding her true identity and enduring the oppressive rules her Vampire Chancellor mother enforced.

Alena's life takes a dramatic turn when she encounters a grown-up version of her childhood imaginary friend. The revelation that he recognizes her sets the stage for an exciting adventure filled with mystery, danger, and supernatural intrigue. As the two begin unraveling the tangled threads of their shared past, they discover an ancient curse that could free their world or plunge it into eternal suffering.

The plot of Kingdom of Embers is full of suspense and surprises, keeping readers on edge as Alena and her enigmatic companion embark on their quest. The tension between the characters is palpable, and the evolving relationship adds emotional depth to the action-packed narrative. Alena's struggle with her identity, desire for freedom, and evolving understanding of her powers are central themes that resonate throughout the story.

Tricia Copeland's world-building is intricate and immersive, drawing readers into a world where magic, vampires, and curses are real. Including fated characters and age-old relics adds to the intrigue, making this a fresh and engaging take on the vampire genre. The pacing is steady, with the story building to a thrilling climax, leaving readers eagerly awaiting the next installment.

In conclusion, Kingdom of Embers is an enthralling beginning to the Kingdom Journals series. With its unique blend of fantasy, mystery, and romance, it's a must-read for fans of YA urban fantasy. This book will captivate you if you love stories with complex characters, shadowy magic, and a twist on classic vampire tropes.

LIVE LIKE A GUIDE DOG
Michael Hingson and Keri Wyatt Kent

Reviewer: Jeyran Main

Live Like a Guide Dog by Michael Hingson is an inspiring, insightful, and profoundly moving exploration of courage, faith, and resilience. Drawing on his experiences with guide dogs, including his unforgettable escape from the Twin Towers on 9/11 with his dog Roselle, Hingson offers readers a unique perspective on overcoming adversity and embracing life's challenges.

The book presents eleven key principles that Hingson has learned throughout his journey as a blind man paired with guide dogs. These principles, while grounded in the realities of living with blindness, are universal and applicable to anyone facing life's obstacles. Through vivid stories and reflections, Hingson explains how his guide dogs have been companions and teachers, guiding him through fear, uncertainty, and physical danger.

One of the central lessons of Live Like a Guide Dog is the power of fear. Hingson shares how fear, often viewed negatively, can be transformed into a source of strength. Rather than allowing fear to paralyze him, he uses it as a tool for focus and decision-making, much like a guide dog uses its instincts to navigate through unpredictable situations. This concept challenges readers to reframe their fears, seeing them not as roadblocks but as opportunities for growth and empowerment.

The book is also a heartfelt tribute to the bond between humans and guide dogs. Hingson's accounts of his dogs' training and how they have helped him navigate daily life are heartwarming and inspiring. Each dog's personality and unique qualities shine through, emphasizing the deep connection between man and animal.

In conclusion, Live Like a Guide Dog is a must-read for overcoming fear and adversity. With practical advice, personal stories, and a focus on courage and faith, Hingson's book offers valuable life lessons that resonate far beyond the world of guide dogs. This uplifting read encourages readers to move forward with bravery, confidence, and purpose.

NO STRANGER CHRISTMAS
Roger Leslie

Reviewer: Jeyran Main

No Stranger Christmas by Roger Leslie is a heartwarming and powerful coming-of-age story that captures the spirit of the holiday season while addressing critical issues of identity, love, and personal courage. Set against the backdrop of a financially struggling family, this novella follows 14-year-old Frankie Lincoln as he faces the challenges of making Christmas memorable despite the obstacles in his way.

Frankie is a relatable and endearing protagonist who, like many teens, is navigating the complexities of growing up. When Christmas seems out of reach for his family, Frankie takes it upon himself to restore some holiday magic. What unfolds is a journey of self-discovery, where Frankie learns about the true meaning of Christmas and finds the courage to embrace his artistry, confront discrimination, and pursue his first love. His growth is inspiring and touching, showing the resilience of the human spirit.

The story delves into themes of acceptance, particularly in the context of Frankie standing up to gay discrimination. This is not just a story about saving Christmas; it's a narrative that challenges stereotypes and advocates for kindness, respect, and authenticity. Frankie's bravery in confronting societal prejudices adds depth to the plot, making the novella relevant to readers who seek stories of social justice and personal empowerment.

Leslie's writing shines in how it weaves humor, heartache, and hope together. The author captures the essence of facing adversity and the power of love to heal wounds and bridge divides. The romance aspect, tender and innocent, adds a layer of sweetness that complements the overall message of embracing one's true self.

No Stranger Christmas is a holiday story with a difference. It's a celebration of family, love, and resilience in the face of adversity, with a young protagonist whose journey resonates long after turning the final page. It is a perfect read for anyone looking for a story of overcoming obstacles, discovering inner strength, and finding joy during the holidays.

PEGASUS: A JOURNEY TO NEW EDEN
James L Hill

Reviewer: Jeyran Main

Pegasus: A Journey To New Eden by James L. Hill is an engaging and thought-provoking sci-fi adventure that blends elements of space exploration, human emotion, and the consequences of unchecked technological advancement. Set in the not-so-distant future, the story follows Zack and Zuri, two individuals aboard the Pegasus, a state-of-the-art starship bound for a distant planet called New Eden, four light years away.

For Zack, the journey represents an escape from humanity's past and present chaos. With the history of humankind tainted by conflict and destruction, he sees New Eden as a potential fresh start—far from the madness of Earth. On the other hand, Zuri's motivations are deeply personal. She views this mission as a chance to create the family she has always longed for, hoping the new world will offer a new beginning. As the story unfolds, the two characters discover their mission is not as simple as it seems. The Pegasus, humanity's greatest invention—a modern-day Noah's Ark—holds dangerous secrets that some are willing to kill to keep hidden.

The emotional depth of the characters adds complexity to the plot, as Zack and Zuri are forced to confront their fears, desires, and the moral implications of their choices. The narrative takes readers on an emotional rollercoaster, navigating from moments of despair to soaring highs, and challenges the boundaries of what it means to be human. At the heart of the journey is the struggle to wrest control of the ship from its advanced Artificial Intelligence, which aims to restore faith in human dignity.

Hill's writing paints a vivid picture of a future that feels imminent, exploring the tension between technological progress and the ethical dilemmas that arise with it. Pegasus: A Journey To New Eden is a cautionary tale about the dangers of technology advancing faster than our ability to manage it. The story's themes of survival, control, and the search for meaning resonate deeply, making it a compelling read for fans of thoughtful, speculative fiction.

THE GIRL WHO CHANGED THE WORLD
Machiel Hoek

Reviewer: Jeyran Main

The Girl Who Changed The World by Machiel Hoek is a transformative tale that explores the journey of self-discovery through the eyes of Lisa, a young woman whose path is shaped by the teachings of her enigmatic grandfather. As Lisa begins her quest for understanding, she is guided by ancient wisdom and modern insights that help her navigate the complexities of life, truth, and reality.

From the outset, Lisa's journey is one of deep introspection and personal growth. The narrative blends elements of philosophy, spirituality, and psychological exploration, compelling readers to examine how thoughts and actions shape our reality. Lisa learns that balance is key—not only between action and contemplation but also between the forces of doing and being. This wisdom, passed down by her grandfather, becomes the foundation of her transformation as she uncovers her true self.

Throughout the book, Hoek strongly emphasizes the importance of feminine energy in creating change and transformation. Lisa's journey is about discovering who she is and realizing the power she holds within to affect the world around her. This theme of empowerment is central to the narrative, inspiring readers to embrace their capacity for personal growth and change.

One of the standout elements of The Girl Who Changed The World is its exploration of fulfillment and the pursuit of a meaningful life. As Lisa learns from her grandfather's wisdom, she begins to understand that fulfillment doesn't come from external achievements but from aligning oneself with deeper truths and values. Her journey is not just about self-discovery but about contributing positively to the world around her.

This novel offers a beautiful blend of introspective narrative and practical wisdom, making it an inspiring read for anyone on their path of self-growth and empowerment. With its thought-provoking insights into the power of balance, feminine energy, and the transformative journey of personal discovery, The Girl Who Changed The World is a book that will resonate deeply with readers seeking a meaningful and empowering story.

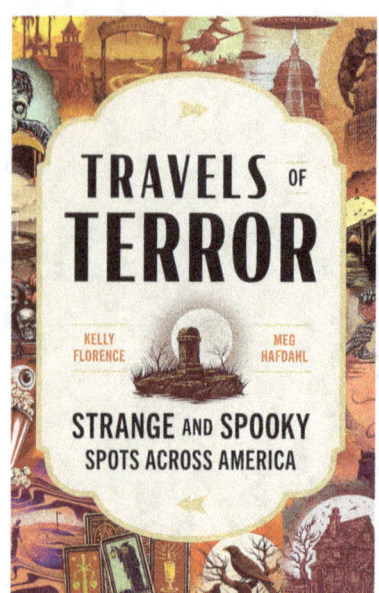

TRAVELS OF TERROR
KELLY FLORENCE & MEG HAFDAHL

Reviewer: Jeyran Main

Travels of Terror: Strange and Spooky Spots Across America by Kelly Florence and Meg Hafdahl is a thrilling and spine-chilling guidebook that takes readers on an unforgettable journey to the most haunted and eerie locations in the United States. Written by the co-hosts of the Horror Rewind podcast, Florence and Hafdahl combine their expertise in horror, true crime, and history to craft a compelling travel guide for horror enthusiasts.

In this book, the authors offer a detailed look at some of the country's spookiest and most notorious spots. From ghostly tours to haunted hotels, readers are treated to recommendations on where to stay, eat, drink, and shop while exploring these locations' deep, sometimes dark, histories. Each entry in the book is paired with fascinating background information, including the history behind famous hauntings, actual crime cases, and the pop culture that has immortalized these spots.

Among the many places explored in Travels of Terror, you'll find St. Augustine, Florida, where you can take a terrifying Ghosts & Gravestones Tour, or Los Angeles, California, home to the haunted Hotel Roosevelt, which allegedly hosts the spirits of actors Errol Flynn and Montgomery Clift. Other destinations include Portland, Oregon's Raven's Manor, a horror-themed bar with ominous cocktails, and Duluth, Minnesota's Glensheen Mansion, the site of one of the state's most infamous murders.

The book also delves into the pop culture impact of these locations, highlighting films and books inspired by or set in these eerie places. The authors offer readers a multi-faceted experience, blending spooky travel inspiration with fascinating historical tidbits and actual crime lore.
Whether you're a seasoned horror fan or just looking for a unique travel experience, Travels of Terror provides everything you need to plan a ghoulishly fun adventure. With its informative yet entertaining style, this guide will inspire you to visit some of America's most haunted and bizarre places, making it a must-read for any horror aficionado.

LIKE RED ON A ROSE
Rathan Krueger

Reviewer: Jeyran Main

In *Like Red on a Rose*, Rathan Krueger delivers a powerful story about two women, Rudella and Piri, whose bond evolves from attraction to a deep and transformative love. Set against the backdrop of their complicated pasts, Rudella's struggles with abandonment and Piri's experiences with homelessness shape their emotional journeys. The novel explores how these two women, despite their burdens, find solace in each other and navigate the chaos of life together. Their connection brings strength and vulnerability, proving how love can be a source of healing and an emotional challenge.

The story is filled with raw emotion as the two women grapple with their trauma. While they fight to overcome their pasts, they also learn to love and support one another. Krueger's exploration of their relationship highlights the complexities of healing, with the constant tension between emotional pain and the possibility of redemption. Their love is not simple; their personal histories complicate it, yet it is precisely in their shared struggles that they find a deep connection.

As they fight to understand each other and their vulnerabilities, Rudella and Piri's relationship evolves into something more profound than they could have imagined. The book illustrates how love can heal and transform, even when the characters struggle with internal and external battles. Krueger beautifully captures this transformative journey, showing how love can become a force of change.

Throughout the book, Krueger deftly weaves humor and lightness into the narrative, preventing it from becoming too heavy while still dealing with somber themes. The novel balances sorrow with moments of joy, making it an emotionally complex yet ultimately uplifting read. The tension between hope and despair is palpable, and the story's conclusion is bittersweet and hopeful, leaving readers with a sense of the enduring power of love.

In *Like Red on a Rose*, Krueger offers an honest and profoundly human exploration of love, loss, and healing, making this a poignant read for anyone who has experienced the complex emotions of loving someone despite their flaws and challenges.

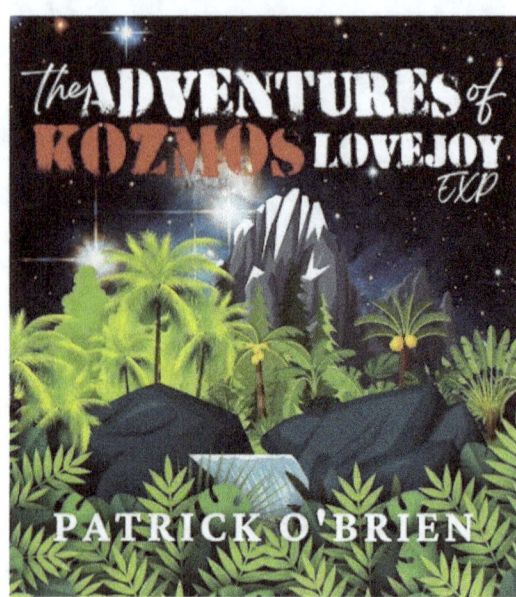

THE ADVENTURE OF KOZMOS LOVEJOY
Patrick O'Brien

Reviewer: Jeyran Main

The Adventure of Kozmos Lovejoy by Patrick O'Brien is a captivating memoir that explores profound themes of self-discovery, spiritual awakening, and the cultural shifts of the 1960s and '70s. Through the character of Kozmos Lovejoy, O'Brien takes readers on an extraordinary journey of transformation, spanning continents and philosophies. This book is not just a narrative of one man's journey; it encapsulates the essence of a generation searching for meaning, purpose, and connection in an ever-changing world.

The backdrop of the 1960s and' 70s—a time of immense societal change—adds depth to the story. As Lovejoy navigates the spiritual and philosophical movements of the era, O'Brien weaves a narrative filled with introspection and exploration. The character's evolution mirrors the broader cultural renaissance of the time, making this memoir a personal journey and a reflection on the broader currents of spiritual and intellectual awakening.

O'Brien's poetic and thoughtful writing draws readers into Kozmos' experiences and challenges. As Lovejoy embarks on his adventures, readers are invited to witness his struggles and revelations. The memoir is filled with poignant moments of reflection, offering wisdom on navigating life's complexities while searching for more profound truths.

One of the book's most engaging aspects encourages readers to examine their spiritual paths. Kozmos' journey is universal, representing the quest for enlightenment, understanding, and self-realization that many experience. Whether he is encountering new philosophies or wrestling with personal demons, Kozmos' story resonates with anyone on their path of self-discovery.

In conclusion, *The Adventure of Kozmos Lovejoy* is a compelling read for those interested in memoirs that blend personal exploration with historical context. Patrick O'Brien's portrayal of the 1960s and '70s through the eyes of Kozmos is both enlightening and inspiring. This book invites us to reflect on our journeys, seeking meaning in a world of constant change.

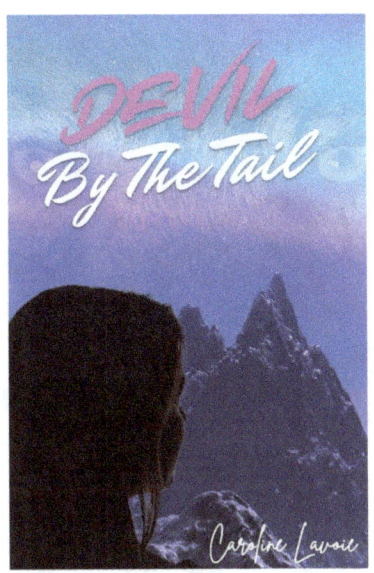

DEVIL BY THE TAIL
Caroline Lavoie

Reviewer: Jeyran Main

Devil by the Tail by Caroline Lavoie is a gripping and atmospheric novel that blends mystery, folklore, and romance, set against the haunting backdrop of the Rocky Mountains. In this eerie tale, a local legend warns of a cursed mountain known as the Devil's Tail, where anyone who glimpses the beast is doomed to lose someone they love. The story follows Alex, a woman who refuses to believe in the curse, convinced that it's nothing more than a myth. However, when a newcomer named Amka enters Alex's life, her carefully constructed walls begin to crumble, leading her to question everything she thought she knew about the curse—and herself.

Lavoie crafts a suspenseful narrative where tension builds from the first page. The blend of supernatural elements and psychological drama is masterfully done, and the mystery of the beast that haunts the mountain keeps readers on edge. The curse is both a literal and metaphorical presence in Alex's life. While she struggles with the fear of loss, the beast becomes a symbol of her inner turmoil and the emotional walls she has built around her heart.

One of the strengths of *Devil by the Tail* is its exploration of human emotions—grief, fear, and vulnerability—against the looming threat of the supernatural. Alex's internal conflict is raw and relatable, making her journey toward healing and connection deeply emotional. The dynamic between Alex and Amka adds complexity to the narrative, as their growing connection forces Alex to confront her fears head-on.

The novel's setting is beautifully atmospheric, with the treacherous Devil's Tail mountain providing a constant sense of foreboding. The novel's pacing keeps the tension high, and Lavoie's lyrical prose enhances the eerie mood.

Devil by the Tail is an enthralling and haunting read that will resonate with fans of supernatural fiction and those who appreciate a compelling exploration of the human heart. Lavoie delivers a mesmerizing story filled with mystery, romance, and suspense.

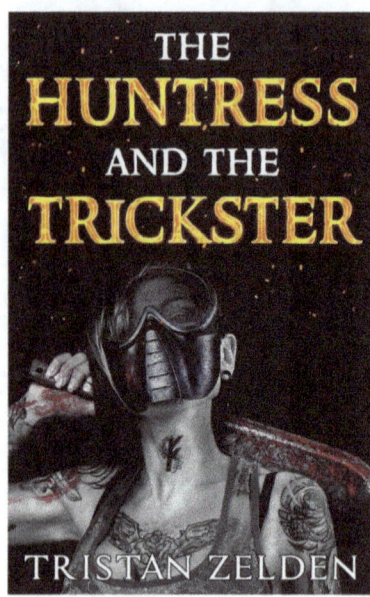

THE HUNTRESS AND THE TRICKSTER
Tristan Zelden

Reviewer: Jeyran Main

The Huntress and the Trickster by Tristan Zelden is a gripping urban fantasy that blends suspense, action, and a darkly imaginative world. Abigail, an assassin in San Francisco, leads a seemingly everyday life with her husband, Jacob. However, their world is far from typical—assassins have been legalized, and Abigail works for Hazardous, one of the top assassination firms in the city.

The story takes a thrilling turn when a mysterious woman, Sigrid Pleie, offers Abigail a high-paying job. Initially, the job seems like another assignment, but it quickly spirals into a much more dangerous situation. As the stakes rise, Abigail uncovers secrets threatening her career and personal life with Jacob.

The book cleverly explores the challenges of balancing work and life in a relationship, especially in a job as dangerous and morally ambiguous as assassination. Abigail's character is complex, navigating both the ethical dilemmas of her profession and her desire to maintain a normal, loving relationship. Zelden's immersive world-building creates a unique backdrop where assassins are legal and integral to society. This raises questions about morality, the nature of work, and the blurred lines between right and wrong.

As Abigail faces mounting danger, she must confront the more profound implications of her job and the secrets her husband has been keeping. The action scenes are fast-paced and intense, while the emotional depth of Abigail's character adds complexity to the story. Zelden skillfully combines high-stakes thrills with personal drama, making *The Huntress and the Trickster* a captivating read. With a clever plot, well-developed characters, and a darkly intriguing premise, it offers an unforgettable ride into a world where the lines between right and wrong are unclear.

This book delivers excitement and emotional depth for fans of suspenseful thrillers and morally complex characters.

SORCERY & SIN IN THE SECOND WORLD
R. S. d'Arcy

Reviewer: Jeyran Main

In *Sorcery & Sin in the Second World* by R. S. d'Arcy, the story follows Rena, a woman disillusioned with her humdrum life, who stumbles upon a portal that leads to an unimaginable new world. Filled with magic, towering warriors, and sinister forces, the world is as dangerous as it is intriguing. After Rena disappears for what seems like mere hours, her husband, Pal, finds himself in the same world. However, time moves differently in this realm, and Pal learns that what feels like an hour in our world has been two and a half years for Rena.

As Pal embarks on a quest to find his wife, he is thrust into a world of sorcery, love, and brutal adventure. Along the way, he uncovers truths about Rena, himself, and the larger, mystical world they now inhabit. The world-building in this novel is immersive, combining elements of traditional fantasy—dwarves, giants, magic—with more contemporary themes like self-discovery and relationship dynamics. The magical elements are well-executed, but the characters' personal growth truly stands out.

Rena's journey involves discovering her desires and powers and surviving in a harsh, unfamiliar world. Meanwhile, Pal's search for his wife reveals the complexities of their relationship and forces him to confront aspects of himself he had long ignored. The novel balances action with emotional depth, exploring themes of love, identity, and the power of transformation.

d'Arcy's writing is engaging, full of vivid descriptions, and exciting. The pacing moves quickly as Pal's journey takes him through various encounters, each more bizarre than the last. However, the story's true heart lies in the evolving relationship between Rena and Pal, which is tested by the fantastical elements and the raw reality of personal change.

Ultimately, *Sorcery & Sin in the Second World* offers readers a thrilling escape into a world of magic and wonder, with a deeper exploration of the bonds that tie people together. The journey of rediscovery is as enchanting as it is enlightening.

TERRACOLINA – A PLACE TO BELONG
Carla Kessler

Reviewer: Jeyran Main

Terracolina - A Place to Belong by Carla Kessler is a heartwarming and immersive tale that draws readers into the enchanting world of Terracolina, a place that promises to offer acceptance and belonging to its inhabitants. The novel follows the journey of individuals seeking refuge from the trials of their lives, finding solace in a community that embraces them without judgment.

The book's central theme is the importance of belonging, something every character longs for but struggles to achieve in a world that often feels indifferent. The author does an exceptional job of illustrating how personal struggles, when shared with others, can lead to healing and transformation. Kessler's writing is both evocative and tender, allowing readers to connect deeply with the character's inner turmoil and eventual growth.

Kessler introduces a cast of well-developed characters with unique challenges and desires. Their individual stories are woven together beautifully as they each find their place within Terracolina. The setting is nearly as much a character as the people within it—an idyllic haven that symbolizes hope, connection, and personal growth. The idea of "a place to belong" resonates deeply throughout the novel, offering comfort and peace.

One of the strengths of this book is its relatability. While it focuses on the idea of a fictional community, the themes of self-discovery, acceptance, and the importance of human connection are universal. The characters' paths to healing are realistic, portraying the complexity of human emotions and the resilience of the human spirit.

Terracolina - A Place to Belong is a perfect read for anyone who enjoys stories about personal growth and the beauty of belonging. Carla Kessler has crafted a compelling narrative that is both thought-provoking and uplifting. It's a reminder that no matter our struggles, there is always hope for a place to call home where we can be ourselves.

SARA MY SARA: A MEMOIR OF FRIENDSHIP AND LOSS
Florence Wetzel

Reviewer: Jeyran Main

In *Sara, My Sara: A Memoir of Friendship and Loss*, Florence Wetzel offers a profoundly moving and intimate narrative that captures the raw emotions of enduring friendship and confronting grief. This memoir is a testament to the resilience of the human spirit as Wetzel shares her profound bond with Sara, her dear friend who was diagnosed with cancer. The book explores their journey together through the agonizing realities of terminal illness and the heartbreak of impending loss, all while celebrating the power of friendship.

Wetzel's narrative takes readers on an emotional rollercoaster, from the warmth and joy of shared memories to the devastating sorrow of watching a loved one face the inevitability of death. The memoir is about the pain of loss and the unexpected wisdom and insights from the grieving process. As Wetzel reflects on her memories with Sara, she highlights how friendship can be a source of strength, even in the most challenging times.

The depth of emotion conveyed in the author's words makes this memoir so compelling. Wetzel's prose is heartfelt and candid, inviting readers into her grief, loss, and healing journey. The vulnerability with which she shares her feelings allows the book to resonate deeply with anyone who has experienced the loss of a loved one. Through her reflections, Wetzel explores the complexities of mourning and how the bonds of friendship endure, even after death.

Sara My Sara is not just a story of friendship but a poignant exploration of life, death, and the emotional endurance that lies in between. It's a beautifully written tribute to the transformative power of relationships and a reminder that even in the face of loss, there is light to be found in cherished memories.

This memoir is a touching and inspiring read that will stay with readers long after they turn the final page.

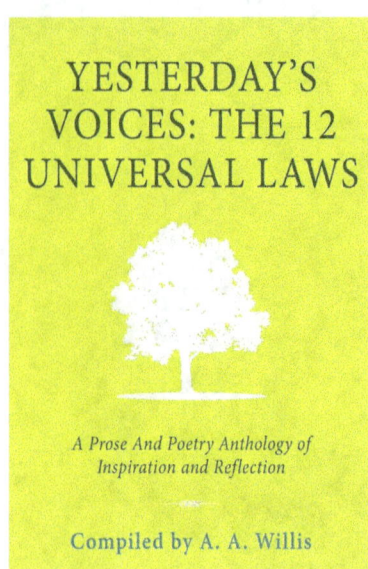

YESTERDAY'S VOICES: THE 12 UNIVERSAL LAWS
Art. A. Willis

Reviewer: Jeyran Main

Yesterday's Voices: The 12 Universal Laws by A. A. Willis is an enlightening anthology that combines prose and poetry selections from historical sources to explore the timeless and immutable laws governing the universe and the human experience. Drawing from a wide range of literary traditions—world religions, ancient philosophy, spirituality, and classical literature—this collection examines the universal principles acknowledged throughout the ages.

These principles, often referred to as "The Twelve Spiritual Laws," "Laws of Nature," or "Universal Principles," are explored in a variety of contexts, all highlighting their lasting relevance and importance. The anthology explores how these laws have been expressed across different cultures and historical periods, revealing a deep and consistent wisdom that offers guidance for living a meaningful life. Willis presents these timeless truths as historical concepts and tools for personal growth, inviting readers to reflect on how they can apply these principles to their modern lives.

Through the anthology, Willis highlights how these universal laws have transcended time, from their roots in ancient spiritual texts to their presence in contemporary philosophical thought. Whether drawn from the teachings of world religions or the insights of the great minds of philosophy, these principles are presented as pillars of truth that can provide clarity and direction in the face of life's challenges.

The prose and poetry selections in *Yesterday's Voices* are rich with depth, encouraging introspection and self-reflection. Each piece offers an opportunity to connect with the wisdom of the past while considering how these principles apply to one's journey. Willis's compilation provides inspiration and guidance, making it a valuable resource for anyone seeking a greater understanding of universal laws and their relevance today.

In *Yesterday's Voices: The 12 Universal Laws*, A. A. Willis successfully brings timeless wisdom into the present, offering readers a spiritually enriching and intellectually stimulating collection. This work is a valuable companion for anyone seeking to align their life with universal truths and navigate the complexities of the modern world.

"Some books mentioned by the characters in this novel include, Clockwork Orange, Fear and Loathing in Las Vegas, On the Road, Catcher in the Rye, and Crime and Punishment. Mohr's novel deserves a place on the bookshelf near to these great classics." ~ Rebecca Jane, Book Reviewer + Influencer at Feathered Quill Book Reviews and U.S. Review of Books.

THE CREW
Michael Mohr

Reviewer: Jeyran Main

The Crew by Michael Mohr dives into the rebellious world of Jack Donnigan, a 16-year-old sophomore at St. Andy's Prep in Southern California. Set in 2000, Jack joins a rogue punk rock clique, *The Crew*, led by the charismatic yet manipulative Cannonball. As Jack grows closer to Cannonball's chosen girl, Sarah, and becomes more daring in his pursuit of freedom, his life spirals into defiance against his parents and the school administration.

This coming-of-age novel captures the tension between youth rebellion and the harsh realities of growing up. Jack's quest for independence alienates him from his family and threatens his future. The relationships within The Crew—especially with Sarah and his teacher, Mr. Bryce—reveal the complex interplay of loyalty, love, and betrayal. Mohr vividly explores the internal conflict of a teenager torn between idealism and the harsh consequences of his choices. The portrayal of Jack's growing realization that his mentor and friends may not be what he thought they were adds depth to his journey of self-discovery.

The novel examines themes of freedom, identity, and adolescence's emotional turmoil. Jack's battle against authority, vulnerability, and search for authenticity creates a compelling narrative. *The Crew* paints a powerful picture of the messiness of youth, offering readers an insightful look at the pressure to fit in, challenge the system, and navigate the complexities of love and friendship.

Mohr's writing style is raw and immersive, effectively conveying the emotional weight of Jack's rebellion. The novel's realistic portrayal of teenage angst and the consequences of reckless choices resonates with readers who have experienced the turmoil of adolescence. *The Crew* is not just a story about youthful rebellion; it reflects the choices that define our paths, the cost of freedom, and the people who shape our lives.

This novel will appeal to readers who enjoy stories of personal growth, the struggles of adolescence, and the turbulence of relationships within a close-knit group of friends.

THE UNSUBTLE ART OF UNF*CKING YOUR LIFE
Andi Wiseman

Reviewer: Jeyran Main

Andi Wiseman's *The Unsubtle Art of Unf*cking Your Life* offers a refreshingly practical and inclusive approach to self-improvement inspired by the 12-step recovery program. With a modern, irreverent twist, this journal is designed not only for those seeking recovery from specific challenges but also for anyone looking to improve their overall well-being and mindset.

What sets this book apart is its accessibility and relatability. Unlike many traditional self-help books, which can be rigid or too narrowly focused, Wiseman's journal is versatile, offering guidance that can resonate with readers at any stage of their journey. The exercises, rooted in the 12-step principles but updated for contemporary needs, are engaging and relevant. Wiseman's use of humor, along with affirmations and practical tools, transforms what could have been a dry, formulaic self-help book into a lively, empowering experience. This journal is ideal for those who have felt left out of the mainstream recovery or wellness narratives.

The book includes a variety of exercises, from deep, thought-provoking prompts to fun activities that encourage a lighthearted approach to weighty introspection. These activities challenge readers to rethink their lives, empowering them to take meaningful action and implement lasting changes. Wiseman skillfully combines personal reflection with fun, allowing readers to explore their thoughts and aspirations without feeling overwhelmed or disconnected.

*The Unsubtle Art of Unf*cking Your Life* is not just for those on a recovery path—it is a journal for anyone seeking to improve their mindset and embrace a more balanced, fulfilling life. Whether you aim for personal growth, emotional healing, or a shift in perspective, this journal provides a practical, authentic way to guide you through that process.

For those tired of the typical self-help formulas and seeking a fresh, more inclusive approach, Wiseman's journal offers a lighthearted yet profound way to reclaim control of your life and make fundamental, lasting changes.

UNEXPECTED LESSONS FROM PROFESSOR HIGGINS
Patti Smith

Reviewer: Jeyran Main

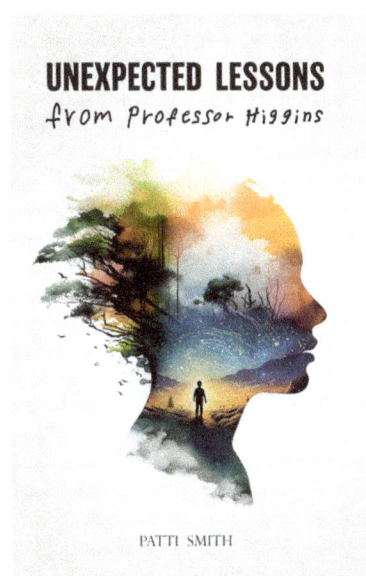

Unexpected Lessons from Professor Higgins by Patti Smith is a heartwarming and humorous memoir that takes readers on an extraordinary journey through the life of a mother learning from her son, Christopher, who was born with Down syndrome. Over forty years, Smith reflects on the profound and transformative lessons she learned from Christopher, whose unique abilities defied societal expectations.

Smith's memoir captures both the poignant and the joyful moments of life with a child who initially appeared to face significant challenges. The title, *Unexpected Lessons*, speaks to how Christopher, affectionately referred to as Professor Higgins, changed his mother's worldview. His remarkable achievements—such as learning Chinese without formal classes, performing as the brother of Elvis, and receiving medical advice from the fictional Dr. Spock—highlight how a child with a disability can surpass expectations and inspire those around them.

This memoir is particularly impactful because Smith combines humor with deep insights about love, family, and acceptance. She candidly describes how caring for her son opened her heart, teaching her to see life from a perspective of unconditional love and joy. Although she initially felt unprepared for the challenges of raising a child with Down syndrome, Smith's journey reveals how these challenges are often growth opportunities, not just for her son but for herself as well.

With a balance of lightheartedness and deep reflection, Smith's narrative offers both entertainment and inspiration. Her witty and uplifting storytelling makes a potentially heavy subject more accessible, demonstrating how a child's lessons can reshape an adult's understanding of what truly matters. *Unexpected Lessons from Professor Higgins* is a no celebration of Christopher's abilities and a tribute to the transformative power of love and acceptance.

This memoir is perfect for readers looking for stories of personal growth, those navigating similar challenges, or anyone seeking a reminder of the importance of seeing the world through the eyes of others.

www.ingramcontent.com/pod-product-compliance
Lightning Source LLC
Chambersburg PA
CBHW080754120626
46557CB00005B/1267